**Spring Magic Life Society, Inc.**

*Abundant Passion, Love, Wisdom, Happiness, Leadership and Success on Purpose...... Coaching, Mentoring, Speaking, Teaching, Mastermind Groups*

# ABUNDANCE TRAIN

## 7 Simple Steps To Abundant Life, Business and Impact

### Spring Zheng

Abundant Entrepreneurship and Thought Leadership Coach

*Empowering Visionary Entrepreneurs and Life Changers to Stand Out as Confident Experts and Leaders in their Ideal Niche with their Unique Gifts!*

www.SpringMagicLife.com

# Contents

## SECTION THREE:

## THE WISDOM AND NEW HORIZON

## SECTION FOUR:

## THE SECRET STRATEGIES AND SYSTEM

## SECTION FIVE:

## YOUR ACTION AND IMPACT

# DEDICATION

To my dearest parents, Zhi Tai Chen and Xian Chong Zheng, who have taught me the first and the most important life lessons and values with genuine love and righteousness, and gave me a beautiful and most cared childhood with all they had in a small town in China.

To my genius husband, Yu Xi Liu, my first and the last love, my lifelong best friend, teacher, comrade and support. I still don't know how to deal with you. To you I am always a blank paper prepared for new discovery and miracles.

To my adorable kids, Ambrose and Athenia, who are my daily reminder about God's angels and the most gracious blessings. You help me grow and become better every day, never lose hope for tomorrow, and embrace new dreams again.

To all the great ancestors, masters and teachers whom I have learned from. Your inspirations and legacies have ignited my imaginations and vision, helped me see all the possibilities, and made my pursuit to greatness not a lonely journey anymore.

And to my faithful God. To you I have only praises and awe, and forever gratitude for the love, purpose, passions, and gifts that you have blessed into me, and for even all the tests and trials you have been guiding me through. I know your abundant presence and glory will always be with me through every breath of my life.

# INTRODUCTION

**Your life is like a fleeting train, instead of wasting it, Turn It into An Abundance!**

Have you just started a new life adventure and cannot wait for the next chapter? Or do you feel that you have tried everything for years but are still staying where you are? No matter which stage you are in your life, career and business, this book will bring you a new start, and to a new height.

The Abundance Train book starts with a story about how a life disaster event related to a train turned into the defining moment of a magical life, the resurrection of a new conscious life, and the start of abundance.

Your genuine and transformative life story is the meaning and the purpose of your life. It points out where you are going, and what you will fulfill. And it becomes the fruit of your life that makes it worth living, worth sharing, and worth being remembered.

But this is not just a story book. It is a book for enlightenment and empowerment. It is aimed to lift up visionary entrepreneurs and life changers, who are meant to impact, change and transform many more lives. Spring Zheng takes you through the top emotional and mindset blocks and breakthroughs, then the 7-step Abundance Code system to create your abundant life, business and impact.

It is designed to create a ripple effect, to call up and equip those experts and thought leaders, to free their emotions and minds, to empower them to confidently step up and stand out in their ideal niche with their unique gifts, and to help them do what they love strategically. In this way, their messages can reach more of their ideal audiences, their voices can be heard by more dream clients, and their lives and businesses will become more successful and fulfilling.

Be prepared, because you will positively impact the world with more energy and power, and together we can accomplish the greatest mission for the abundance of all.

# Who Can Benefit Most From the Abundance Train

The following Visionary and Purposeful people will find this Book enlightening and empowering as they are ready to discover and align with their true purpose, passions and gifts, unleash their greater inner powers, do what they love strategically to create a lucrative business and meaningful impact in the world, and fulfill an abundant life with happiness, confidence, success and freedom.

Visionary Entrepreneurs and Life Changers such as coaches, authors, speakers, consultants, business executives and leaders, you are meant to impact, lead, and change many others' lives, and you are blessed to be the catalyst of positive changes.

It's my dearest calling to create such ripple effects, by empowering more experts and thought leaders to step up for your calling and stand out in the market, so that you can fulfill a more successful life, transform more lives, and together we can accomplish the greatest mission for the abundance of all.

# SECTION ONE:

# THE INNER BATTLES

Every solution starts from a problem. Every problem starts from our inner response.

The majority of this world's problems start from our immature, irresponsible, or unwise thinking, action and response. And every such problem has a solution starting from inside of us. We are the source, the result, and the solution of our problems.

This section starts from our biggest life lessons, which we all may experience in different forms and with which we are still familiar. Some of them may become our life's turning points, or epiphanies. Our life stories often become the best source of our inspirations, growth and strength.

First, I'd like to share with you my transformative life events and stories, where I came from, how and who I became through those defining moments, which contributed to the origin of this book.

Then we'll explore your desires and challenges. Some are common, and some are unique to you.

Only until we fully open ourselves, be honest with ourselves, and look deeply into our life and the events and stories that occurred for us (instead of interpreting them as occurred to us), could we be ready to further explore the code of abundance.

This first section is to help us to be true to each other, as genuine lives, through this book and interaction, so you can be fully true to yourself as well.

# 1. MY RESURRECTION STORY:
# CRUSHED INTO ABUNDANCE

"Love never fails. Live in faith, passions and abundance."

~ *Spring Zheng*

Spoiler alert: this is not a typical life or career or business story, but a genuine love story. I'd share with you from the beginning, as I have learned and believed that every meaningful thing starts from love.

I graduated from one of the best universities in China. My first job was working in the capital city and the biggest bank of China. Everyone told me what I did was impossible for a girl from a small town. And what's next? I became a poet.

His name was the Chinese American boy. He was an exchange student I met in the university cafeteria. We became good friends through many discussions and conversations, and even debates about the US and China. Then when he went back to America, I started writing, so many hundreds of poems and so many hundreds of love letters. All just to preserve the pure friendship with my first love.

For 10 years, I had many men and many boys who came after me as pursuers, including the scary one who waited overnights outside of my apartment building and wrote me a love letter with his blood! I had to call the security guard to send that poor boy away. I rejected them all, because he was my one beautiful love.

During that time, I went against Chinese tradition. We are realists. We don't believe in spirituality. Spirituality is superstition. But during those 10 years, I found an underground family church and I was baptized. I felt God is true love, and He blessed me with my one true love, and for those 10 years the only reason I could survive was my faith in God.

I got accepted to PhD programs at Columbia University and the University of Pennsylvania. Unfortunately my student visa application to America was rejected. I suffered for a few years because of this big turning down of life, dream and opportunity. After I collected my strength again, I started to pursue an Executive MBA program while I was working full time in an international company.

After I graduated with an EMBA, the only way I was able to come to America, was that my true love agreed to marry me. But he married me as a friend, because he loved me like a friend. I didn't care, because he was my one true love. We got married and we had two lovely kids. It was my dream come true.

I found a great job working in a Fortune 100 company's headquarters in downtown Manhattan as a director of performance management. After 5 years, I was not feeling very happy and fulfilled in the corporate world but did not know how to change my situation. During that time, my husband started his own business as an attorney at law and also an investor in real estate.

In 2009, due to the financial crisis in 2009, I lost my job, but I felt relieved and a secret joy for a potential big life change. Through 6 months of deep reflection, career coaching help and research, I decided to leave the corporate world, and follow my calling to start my entrepreneurship as a life and business coach. I called myself a Happiness Coach, to help other people discover and live on their purpose, passions and gifts, and do what they love.

By our late 30's, both of us were entrepreneurs with freedom. We moved to Orlando with our kids, half an hour distance to Disney World. We had a big house on the lake and golf course, an acre of land. Even today I can still clearly remember that time in Orlando. Sometimes, as I looked out of the gigantic windows at our blue swimming pool and the huge crescent lake, I thought, this life looks like heaven on earth. It almost felt too good to be true.

It WAS too good to be true.

I know that every marriage has its problems. My marriage with my husband is no different. Even to this day we have our problems. Things suddenly changed when we were almost touching heaven. We went into a severe faith and marriage crisis. With a broken heart, I had to give up our Orlando home and move to my in-law's house in New York City with two kids. At our lowest, at my lowest, despite my children, and despite my love for him, I did not want to go on.

One night in the winter, after sending the kids to sleep and writing my farewell letters to them, I went down to the Long Island Rail Road. I sent him a text message, which I thought would be my last love message to him, even though I was still hoping he was gonna come and save me.

I climbed down off the platform onto the rail road tracks, and I saw the lights of the train far in the distance, coming towards me. I was terrified. I stood there, and I was terrified. Should I run away? Or can I stay? I have to stay! But what about my children? What about my pain? At least the pain and the nightmare will be over!

I closed my eyes, and tried to have the courage just to stay there, to let the train end the pain. The sound of the train engine and wheels is getting louder and louder and LOUDER. The freezing wind blew through my coat and chilled me to my bones. The train whistle pierced the cold night air. WooooooooWOOOOOOO!

My heart and my breath were frozen by the horror. My whole body was numb and felt as if I was being swallowed under the train. I thought that would be the end of my life story, and the world would be all OVER to me. As the train gets closer and closer, and finally, EEEEEEENNNNNNNDDDDDDD…...

When I opened my eyes, there was the train, stopped, one foot in front of my face, way before the station. At that moment, I realized, what a miracle! God must have some unfinished plan with my life.

That was years ago. Since then, it is my faith in God that has kept me alive and strong… During many dark and lonely nights, I kneeled down on the ground and prayed to God that I could sleep in peace and forgiveness. And as I said, even to this day, me and my husband our relationship still has big gaps. But we have tried to come closer together. We even went and walked on fire with Tony Robbins…

During those darkest years, I lost happiness, but I was resurrected with resilience and abundance, like a phoenix resurrected through fire and ashes… And since then it has totally transformed my life and my coaching practice.

Since that night on the train tracks, I feel I'm living a new life. My love for the world and for God is so much bigger than my old love. I realize I gave ALL of myself and lost myself, when I was only loving one man. I now fully love and believe in myself, and God's mission for me to empower more visionary entrepreneurs to step up for their calling, and stand out in their ideal niche as confident experts and thought leaders with their unique God-blessed gifts, to transform more lives, and positively impact the world for the abundance of all.

The train that almost crushed my life actually brought me into the world of abundance. It's my Abundance Train.

And I thank God for my NEW LIFE!

## 2. MY TWO BIGGEST FEARS

"If you want to conquer fear, don't sit home and think about it.
Go out and get busy."
~ *Dale Carnegie*

I remember at every important life stage, I have had two biggest fears, even though they evolve and change as I grow up.

When I was a little kid back in my small hometown, a rolling mountainous county in Sichuan Province, in the southwestern part of China, my two biggest fears were toothaches and taking the bus. Because during that time China did not have advanced hygiene habits and health care facilities, I had cavities and toothaches, and was very afraid of going to visit the dentists because whatever they did was painful. That fear slowly ceded when I grew older and all my teeth problems were fixed.

My second fear in my childhood was to take a bus to visit any bigger city outside of my hometown. My hometown was so small and had very genuine country lifestyle. We walked to school, working places, parks, or anywhere else in dozens of minutes. We did not even see bicycles. We only had a long-distance bus station where people took buses to other towns and cities which took hours of traveling. I would get car sick through the whole journey and vomit quite a few times when occasionally I needed to go outside with my parents. So taking a bus was my another big fear, until I left my hometown and went to a big city to attend university, where I learned to ride a bicycle and take buses often.

When I grew into adulthood, I had two new fears. One was swimming because of my fear of water and drowning. I only learned how to swim 5 meters in my university as our Physical Education required and gave us an annual learning opportunity. And for those 5 meters I was holding my breath with my head all submersed in the water. I dared not to try to get back into water till I gave birth to two kids and I had to encourage them to learn swimming from scratch. I was glad that with their baby steps, I also got the courage to learn step by step and eventually could swim a whole lap. I finally could enjoy water with a sense and feeling like a fish!

My second fear in adulthood was to drive in New York City. I got my first driver's license in Beijing China learning with cars with manual transmission. After I got to New York, the crazy traffic frightened me. With daily commute to Manhattan and little kids at home to care for, plus my husband would drive us during weekends, I found excuses not to drive.

I gained my driver's license in the US when we were in Orlando where there's no requirement for parallel parking. I still collected a lot of courage to dare to drive on highway when I needed to send my husband to the airport right after I got my driver's license. After we moved back to New York City, for the majority of the time, I needed to send my kids to their activities. With practice, I finally grew into a good driver in the Big Apple.

I feel that life has been the best teacher that pushes us forward and holds us accountable to learn, grow and become independent. All those fears that I once thought would last forever eventually became history and memory. Now when I am recalling those early memories, while laughing at myself, I really appreciate how far I have grown through.

Before I got my faith in God, I was afraid of darkness and all kinds of ghosts or evil spirits people told in stories or showed in movies, especially when I was a child. After my soul was enlightened by God, there were no more ghosts nor their shadows in my mind or imagination.

Before and during my marriage crisis, I was afraid of losing my husband and our love. After going through the longest and darkest tunnel and life's resurrection, I walked out of that fear as well, and stepped into abundant love for myself and all others.

Now in my mature adulthood, as an entrepreneur, and an abundant life and business coach, do I have any fears? I thought I had no more fears.

Some of you may say: public speaking! Yes, showing up and speaking in the public is many people's big fear. It did make me very nervous, too, especially at the beginning of my coaching when I was totally unconfident in my English as my second speaking language. But I was also excited whenever I could get a chance to talk in public.

I have been challenging myself to show up and speak up, in front of small groups, in front of events, in front of the camera, in front of Facebook Live … little by little, I'm not that nervous any more, and I do not worry about my English speaking anymore, because I have been focusing more on the content and value that I could provide to others.

When you put the benefits of others higher than what you would look like or sound like to others, you could eventually overcome the fear or nervousness on public speaking. I even challenged myself to not put on any makeup and show up genuinely on Facebook for more than one year! So public speaking is more of a thrilling and fun challenge to me than fear.

I was taking a 30-day One Funnel Away Challenge with Russell Brunson and his team of coaches. They challenged attendees to crush our fears and false beliefs. I took the challenge to reflect deeply into my mind and heart. Instead of real fears, I found my two dilemma false beliefs that had been preventing me from bigger achievements.

How many of you are really looking forward to success?

Are some of you afraid of being very successful?

I thought more success means more sacrifice. Being more successful will cost me more time on business and serving others so it will reduce my quality time with my family, with my kids, even with myself. My freedom, my health and my flexibility will all be squeezed by more success. More success means more responsibility and commitment to serving other people.

I have a dream that someday I could be in front of many people every day to teach and empower them, and share the speaking stage with my favorite mentor and role model Tony Robbins to impact millions.

But at the same time, I worried that if I become that successful, I would not have personal time anymore, my life would belong to the masses, and my life would be serving the public every day nonstop. Every day I would be expected to be busy, share great messages, and work at my high or peak performance. That does not look like a fancy picture to me!

So because of such negative picture of big success, unconsciously it's been dragging me away from putting forth all my efforts and greatest commitment. I am not one hundred and ten percent in the business development.

On the other hand, I do not want to fail. Nobody wants to fail. Many entrepreneurs and business owners have a fear of failure. Many small failures could already break people's hearts especially if they are working on their passions.

I've had many small failures through the 10 years of coaching practice. For example, some offers did not sell well, quite a few funnels did not work effectively, some marketing campaigns did not get a good response, many speaking sessions did not attract enough eyeballs, quite some sales conversations did not convert......almost every day you could count some result-less effort as a failure. It is heart breaking. And unavoidably you may ask yourself, what if in the end I will fail after all these efforts? It's a devastating thought for which many of us could not find a good answer.

So these two worries are fighting with each other inside of me, worrying about being too successful would require my sacrifice and lose my freedom, and worrying about not being successful in realizing what I would achieve and fulfilling my purpose, which would be a failure of my life.

I wrote these two dilemma thoughts down and started to work on them.

I knew they were my false beliefs. I need to find replacing and greater beliefs.

I started to have more focused and closer observation on those super successful ones. For example Tony Robbins, Russell Brunson, Brendon Burchard, Opera Winfrey, Marie Forleo, Dean Graziosi, Kim and Robert Kiyosaki, etc.

From the outside, they are super busy, they do not have much personal time, and they do not have freedom like that of a normal person. It's all in our imagination from outsiders who have not achieved that kind of success.

We did not see the quality. Quality of their freedom, quality of their time and value, quality of their environment and lifestyle, quality of the people in their lives, quality of the new opportunities that are attracted into their lives every day, and quality of their happiness and fulfillment!

Those successful ones also have greater mastery and control of their lives. They have healthier lifestyle and habits than normal people. They are much healthier and strong than people in their similar age. They developed much better self-discipline capabilities than the majority of other people. They are more productive with higher level performance, better time management and efficiency, which creates more quality time for them to share with their loved ones.

Compared with their life and business mastery, I have a long way to catch up! My original imagination and worry are all false beliefs that are not doing me any good.

Now, about the other dilemma, my worry about failure, the number one fear of the majority of people.

It's time to remind myself, and compare me with myself from ten years ago. In 2009, when I just got into the coaching industry, and all I had was just my newly clarified purpose and my passion.

Ten years later, I am still holding the similar purpose and passion, but see what I have now. I have 10 years of experiences with all the ups and downs, celebrations and lessons, great progress and mistakes. I have a stronger mindset and emotional maturity. I have a clearly focused niche and I know exactly who my ideal clients are. I have my business system and great offers. I have my community and followers. I have my platforms, and most importantly, I have never given up and have built so many small milestones that I could count and be grateful.

I have developed such mindset that success and fulfillment is a journey, not a destination. The growth through this journey is the most meaningful and enjoyable part. The personal growth and the person I'm becoming is the most rewarding success from this entrepreneurial journey.

Many entrepreneurs and business owners compare themselves with others, with their peers, with successful ones, especially those "overnight" successful ones, and they may become frustrated and start sabotaging themselves. Self judgement only makes it more difficult. The things between your ears, your thoughts, are your most challenging enemies.

Every step forward, if you are growing compared with yourself from yesterday, it is a success. Abundance thinking is not about achieving success and abundance at the end of the journey, but about every day learning, growing, creating, giving, serving and providing value.

If you are growing, your dream is expanding, you are driven by your passion, you are moving your business forward, and you become more skillful and more resilient. Your stepping stones paved toward your bigger vision and dream are your measurable success already.

Such internal reflection and homework has helped me solve the dilemma false beliefs and conflicts inside of me, and make me feel unstoppable on the ongoing journey of pursuing my dreams, serving others, and fulfilling the special call to my life.

In the following chapters, let's explore your desires, challenges and the opportunities, and the wisdom on how to invite abundance into the core of your life and business.

## 3. YOUR DESIRES AND CHALLENGES

*"The purpose of life is to discover your gift.*
*The work of life is to develop it.*
*The meaning of life is to give your gift away."*
*~ David Viscott*

When you pursue anything in life, what do you want to fulfill the most?

I believe it's not just for a higher educational degree, a learning experience, a shining title, a new adventure, a business to earn money, better relationships, a better working or living environment. There must be some deeper desires that drive you to develop yourself, look for new opportunities, pursue new things, and much more beyond.

We all want a broader horizon and brighter future, which our current mind could not even imagine. Our life would not stop and stay where we are. Our lives are called to fulfill something bigger than us.

## You Are Special

As you have acquired and are reading this book Abundance Train, I believe you have special pursuits, and you have stood out of most mediocre people who would rather stay in their comfort zone or tolerate their status quo mostly because of their fears to take on challenges and make changes.

I know you are such a special person who is conscious and visionary, open to and curious of life's full potential and deeper meaning, who is ambitious, loving learning, passionate, taking initiatives, seeking success, and willing to take ownership of your destiny.

You are not just a dreamer and thinker, but also a doer and creator. You do not just want to play always as a member and follower, but also desire to be a leader in your specialized area. You may have a strong entrepreneurship and independent spirit, be most time practical, strategic, and also risk taking with a reasonable analysis.

You would do what you love and create a purposeful, successful and sustainable business that you can leave as a legacy. You can't wait to claim your own niche and expertise, make a big difference in both your own life and those lives whom you desire to serve with your best gifts!

If this is you, you can proudly call yourself **a Visionary Creator!**

## The Primary Concerns and Challenges

Through articles, online search engines, and research conducted by coaches and career service organizations, we learned about what the majority of professionals, MBAs, entrepreneurs and business owners are concerned about or even worrying about most of the time.

### Questions Often Asked:

- What am I really passionate about? What do I want to do the most in life?
- I'm not clear about my life's purpose. What direction should I focus on?
- I'm discovering the gap between my ambition and reality, how do I overcome the gap and realize my dream?
- How can I do what I love and also make a decent living?
- What critical decisions should I make and what opportunities should I catch to make the best of my life?
- I'm feeling unhappy or even miserable in my current life and career. Where should I start first for a breakthrough?
- How to start or transition into a career and business that I would love to do and also succeed?
- How to balance my busy work schedule with a life that I can enjoy every day?
- How to build up the best network and resources to support my success?
- I am getting a new degree in education and I like the ideas of startup or entrepreneurship, what's next for my ideal life and where to start?

- How to live my best life with happiness, confidence, wealth and impact?
- I have started a business, but not fulfilled yet, what should I do better?
- I've had a business for a while and have achieved some success, what could be my next level and how to accelerate the growth?
- There are so many great entrepreneurs and business owners in the market, how could I stand out, attract more of my ideal clients and make bigger impact?

Most people are not clear about why they are on Earth (their life's purpose), who they are, and what their passions and gifts are. Some of them want to focus on how to find quick solutions or shortcuts, but they will always end up with bumping into the wall or getting lost somewhere. Starting with how will never get you to where your life is really meant to be.

Some people may know their purpose and passions, but because of the lack of clarity, best strategies and accountability, they often become frustrated by tough reality and give up during the long pursuing journey.

### The Top Four Desires

We learned that most talented people have these top four desires when developing their career and business, and exploring more about life.

***Balance, Prosperity, Passion, and Meaning.***

- **Balance:** What lifestyle should I develop to have a good balance and harmony in both work and life? How to keep the balance when life or business is really challenging and stressful?

- **Prosperity:** How can I do what I love and also get good rewards to prosper in every area of my life, including financial success?

- **Passion:** What is my passion? How to turn my passion into a business that I love to do? How to always live and work with passion and joy without losing it during the process?

- **Meaning:** Who am I? What am I created for? What gifts do I own? What could I do to fulfill the best meaning of my life?

## What Do We Pursue The Most

Only change is constant. Our outside world keeps changing.

Global economy goes up and down and continuously fluctuates which keeps impacting our work and life. It seems to be out of our control. We are such tiny parts of the whole system. It sounds logical that we should just passively follow the big winds of change to survive.

After countless trials and errors, we human beings are developing physically, mentally, emotionally, and spiritually. Eventually some conscious people gained the wisdom and realized that the main challenges are not from outside, but from within ourselves.

Almost everything is about 90% more of **inner game**, which includes your mindset, your beliefs, your spirituality, and your emotional health.

The biggest enlightenment is, we as the **creators**, have the biggest power in changing ourselves to change the world. We can **choose** to have the positive impact or negative impact, from one to many.

The best part is, we all have our own life's purpose, once you discover and start to **live out** your blessed purpose every day, then everything else in your life will be in great alignment.

What do Visionary Entrepreneurs, Life Changers and Business Owners want the most? We find such a shared awakening and pursuit:

**Live a life that is as purposeful, fulfilling and successful as possible!**

### The Primary Mission that We Face

More and more purposeful and visionary entrepreneurs and business owners are finding such a great mission to fulfill their lives:

**Discover my life's purpose, reveal my passions and gifts, do what I love and develop a meaningful business to serve and help others, so that I could realize my life's best values, receive abundant financial rewards, and live a life that is as purposeful, fulfilling and successful as possible.**

*You can never live an abundant life unless you live out your purpose and passions, do what you love strategically and sustainably, and give your best values and gifts to the world.*

# SECTION TWO:

# THE MARKET BATTLES AND NEW WEAPONS

After we have looked truly into our inner battles, and our life's determining events and stories, now let's look beyond ourselves. For visionary entrepreneurs, life changers and business owners, every day we are in the market, and unavoidably we all may notice that there are many invisible battles, without bloodshed and fireworks, but intense enough to bring many of us both pressure and stress.

We'll discuss the Career Death Spiral, and the Number One Business Killer to understand what evil powers are prevailing in the market. But the good news is we will not lose our battles there. We will further share the contrast and triumph that are the Fulfilling Career Spiral and the Key to Business Success.

Every battle has two sides. We will discuss the Top 4 Mistakes that are Blocking You from Realizing Your Dreams. Those are your enemies for life and business success. You know that we will not be stopped there. We'll share the New Mindsets for Your Breakthroughs where you will learn 5 breakthrough mindsets that will help you reveal your inner strength and overcome any obstacles both internally and externally.

This section will further prepare you to stand up as an alert and equipped warrior, to protect yourself from any attack, no matter inside or outside, to be strong enough.

Don't worry, we will not always fight, even though that equipment is necessary. In later sections, we will prepare you to become a creator for the next steps, to create, enjoy and harvest. But first, you need to be able to go through the tunnel and tests, so that we will know that you will not be easily blown away by big winds and storms, on the journey of pursuing and receiving abundance.

# 4. THE CAREER DEATH SPIRAL AND The #1 BUSINESS KILLER

"Too many of us are not living our dreams because we are living our fears."

~ *Les Brown*

Many people are finding themselves stuck in such a career dilemma that they dread going to work before every Monday. Some of them clearly say that they HATE their work, while many of them fear changes, or don't know what to do to change for good.

## The Career Death Spiral

Regardless of whether you are working for employers, or working on your own business, when you are not working on your purpose and passions, most possibly you will dislike or hate your work sooner or later at some level or in some areas, as a result, you will become less engaged.

The less you engage, the less creative you will be. The less creative you will be, the less you can accomplish. The less you accomplish, the less financial rewards and opportunities you may receive, which will cause you further unhappiness. The less you enjoy what you are doing, the worse you will perform.

Such career death spiral will keep dragging you down emotionally, spiritually, mentally and physically, if you don't know how to change the situation and jump out of the downward spiral.

Here below we have the illustration of the Career Death Spiral with more details.

## Career Death Spiral

1. No Purpose and Passion

5. Less Accomplishment

2. Hate What You Do

8. Worse Performance

4. Less Creativity

6. Less Financial Reward & Opportunity

7. Less Happiness

3. Less Engagement

The Career Death Spiral is like this: Not working on your Purpose and Passion will lead to Dislike or Hate for What You Do, which will lead to Less Engagement, then Less Creativity, then Less Accomplishment, then Less Financial Reward and Opportunity, then Less Happiness, then Worse Performance, and so on.

Be aware of and get out of the Career Death Spiral AS SOON AS YOU CAN! Like Herb Brooks said, "*RISK SOMETHING OR FOREVER SIT WITH YOUR DREAMS.*"

Start a process of self discovery and transformation today with good support, to leap into your happy Fulfilling Career Spiral, which is introduced in the next chapter. It'll be worth everything to refresh and restart your career on the right track!

### The #1 Business Killer

Through a long time of coaching practice, I choose to work with my ideal clients: visionary entrepreneurs, life changers and business owners, who have gone through the career dilemma and made the most critical decision to pursue their purpose and passions, do what they love strategically and make differences for themselves, their loved ones, and the people they are serving. This tough decision is really proof of their courage, determination and commitment to their own life and those whom they love. It is the first step towards their business success and personal fulfillment.

It's like in order to get to your desired travel destination, you cannot just dream of or watch from far away, you need to take action by taking a car, train, ship or plane to get there and actually enjoy it. The decision to become an entrepreneur or business owner and to do what you love and start your own business is like taking a journey towards your destination.

Starting your own business, or even starting your own passion business, does not mean you will automatically succeed. Statistics show that, the majority of startups fail, and only a small percentage succeed. The success ratio is only like 10%. And many new startups fail in their first year.

A careful survey of failed startups determined that **42%** of them identified the **"lack of a market need for their product"** as the single biggest reason for their failure. As a result, they will run out of cash and even fail in the first year.

**When there is a purposeful passion and gift, there is a market that needs it.**

We can also say, before those startups launched their product, they did not fully clarify their purpose, passions and gifts. They did not fully understand their ideal market, and did not find the right solution that bridges their purposeful passion, gifts and the right market. Such a match, the central overlap, the sweet spot, is their niche and their best value to the ideal market.

**Missing the critical pre-work on defining their best niche, that integrates their purposeful passion, their genius gifts, their ideal market and their compelling solution, is the Number 1 Killer for most startups.**

The following illustration shows the relationships between your Niche and your Purposeful Passion, your Gifts and Expertise, and your ideal Market Needs and Segments.

# Business Niche & Ideal Market

In our **Purposeful and Profitable Niche Secrets** program, we have in-depth teaching, coaching and exercises to help you clarify your greatest niche, so that you could transform your passion and genius into an abundant niche business. You can check this program out here:

https://coaching.springmagiclife.com/nichesecrets.

# 5. THE FULFILLING CAREER SPIRAL AND THE KEY TO BUSINESS SUCCESS

*"The only way to do great work is to love what you do.*
*If you haven't found it yet, keep looking. Don't settle."*
*~ Steve Jobs*

Contrast to the Career Death Spiral which keeps you drowning, we have the great news of an uplifting and promising career path for you.

### The Fulfilling Career Spiral

When you are doing work on your purpose and passions, you will be good at it, and you will have more engagement. The more you engage, the more you will have creativity. The more creative you are, the more you can accomplish. The more you accomplish, the more financial rewards and promotion opportunities you can receive including taking higher leadership positions. As a result, you will have more enjoyment on your work, which leads to even better performance.

This fulfilling spiral will keep you going up on your career and self realization.

Here below is the illustration of the Fulfilling Career Spiral with more details.

# Fulfilling Career Spiral

6. More Financial Reward and Leadership

2. Good At It

3. More Engagement        5. More Accomplishment

7. More Enjoyment        1. Purpose & Passion

4. More Creativity

8. Better Performance

The Fulfilling Career Spiral is like this: Working on your Purpose and Passion will lead to being Good At It, which will lead to More Engagement, then More Creativity, then More Accomplishment, then More Financial Reward and Leadership, then More Enjoyment, then Better Performance, and so on.

I hope that you now can't wait to get onto your own Fulfilling Career Spiral!

### The Key to Business Success

With only a great purpose and passion, you still could not make a business successful.

We discussed in the last chapter that **missing the critical pre-work on defining your ideal niche: including your purposeful passion, your gifts and expertise, your best solution, and your ideal market, is the Number 1 Killer for most startups.**

In other words, **the key to business success is to first clarify your ideal niche: your purposeful passion, your gifts and strength, your best solution and your ideal market.**

Business success also needs some other important factors. I promise to reveal all the success factors in the following chapters of this book Abundance Train.

The following illustration shows how to find your niche, which is the fundamental success factor for your business.

# Business Niche & Ideal Market ➡ Success

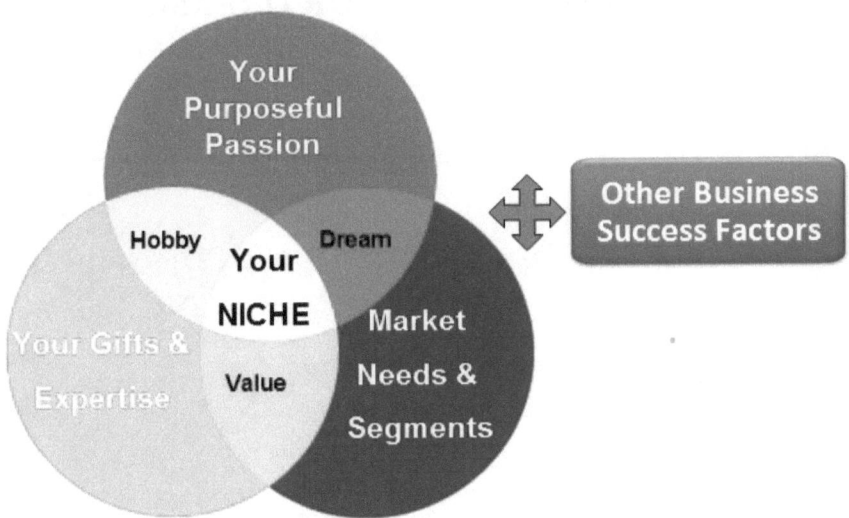

# 6. TOP 4 MISTAKES BLOCKING YOU FROM
# REALIZING YOUR DREAMS

*"MAKE SURE YOUR WORST ENEMY doesn't LIVE*
*BETWEEN YOUR own two EARS."*
*~ Laird Hamilton*

### Top Mistake 1: Mind above Heart

**Jump into Direction and Actions Guided By Your Mind Instead of Your Heart, i.e.**
**Jump into HOW, while lack of clarity on Your Purpose, Passions and Who You Are.**

Many people are not clear about their purpose, passions and directions. As a result, they let the environment and others to choose for them. They jump into trends and allow themselves to be misled by popular things or what others admire.

Many have not learned how to listen to their inner voice and fully discover who they are, why they are here, and what their desires and dreams are. They may let their dreams give way to what society thinks is the best for them. Sometimes they just pursue the most convenient ways or opportunities that come to them first.

Easily pursuing a wrong direction chosen by the mind instead of the heart is the biggest mistake for most people with a big price to pay. The result of not following your true passions is that after initial excitement people would suffer from unsatisfied life and career / business and get stuck there for a long time before a real change happens.

Such paths would be like detours. You could not see it clearly at the beginning, but then you have to walk a long confusing distance to get to where you want to go. It costs people most of their time, money, energy and opportunities. In the worst situation, like we introduced in Chapter 2, you could fall into the trap of Career Death Spiral and the lack of true purpose and passion could kill your business in its early stages.

When one has a lack of clear purpose, passions and who you are, you could have an unavoidable **lack of self worth and confidence**. You may doubt and sabotage yourself from time to time, and could not really get yourself out of negativity and stress. You may also develop some limiting beliefs that become your blind spots of which you could be unaware for a long time.

Many times, when one has a lack of purpose, passions and who you are, you could also easily **allow your past to define your future**. Your past negative experiences could have been blocking you for years from creating a new life with freedom and empowerment.

When people get stuck in their situation or face difficulty in making the right decision, your family or friends may try to help you analyze the situation and make reasonable choices. The best advice you could receive is "**Follow your heart**", instead of: follow your mind. Why? Because we are now understanding more about human minds and thoughts compared with your heart.

Our thoughts often "cheat" or mislead us. According to research, each person has an average of *60,000 THOUGHTS* a day! That's one thought per second in every waking hour! Amazingly, *95* percent are the same thoughts repeated every day. On average, *80* percent of those habitual thoughts are negative.

On the contrary, your heart would not lie to you. Your heart is who you are. It tells you what you are looking for, what you really enjoy and what you do not. There is an ancient Indian proverb: **"Certain things catch your eye, but pursue only those that capture the heart."**

You still need your mind to do logical analysis and help you make decisions, but more importantly, your heart is connected with your purpose and passions and will tell you what you truly enjoy and what you should aim for.

## Top Mistake 2: Unclear Business Niche

**Missing the definition and focus on your sweet-spot business niche and ideal market is the Number 1 Killer for most startups.**

**Business Niche = You + Your Best Solution + Your Ideal Market**

There are normally three kinds of syndromes for unclear business niche.

### 1). Too Broad and Too Generic Business Niche

Most entrepreneurs and business owners would love to serve ALL and ANY people. They are so passionate about their products and programs that they believe they can help all people, or they think they can help a person solve all of life's issues. So they network and do marketing to all and any people. The result is, few people could really connect with their generic language and would invest in their services. Just like a doctor, if he claims that he can heal all people or all your sicknesses, would you choose such a doctor?

### 2). Multiple Business Niches

Some entrepreneurs and business owners have 2 or 3 business niches and markets. They feel they are good at a few solutions to help a few markets. Previously I was trying to help both professionals in the corporate world and entrepreneurs to follow their purpose and passion to do what they love in different path, a professional path and entrepreneurial path.

Through practice, I found that it's challenging to focus on two different paths. That means, I need two sets of programs, marketing, networking, launches, partners, and delivery. It's like a juggler juggling multiple balls, trying to keep the flow and balance.

I eventually chose to focus on serving my ideal market which I love the most and could benefit the most from my purposeful and passionate services: visionary entrepreneurs and business owners who are ready to unleash their purpose and passions, do what they love strategically, and fulfill an abundant life with happiness, confidence, wealth and freedom.

So now everything is clear with a flow. I can build up the best connections and concentrate the best resources and energy to serve this niche market for my clients' best transformations. It's a great choice both for me and for my ideal clients.

## 3). Confused and Shifting Business Niche

Some entrepreneurs and business owners are not sure about their business niche. They are confused themselves or jumping on different new ideas, which you can see from their networking and marketing messages, which could cause confusion to their audience as well, not being sure of who they are serving or what solution they are providing.

Confusion can cause change and shifting as well. Some entrepreneurs may change their focus every few months with different market and different service. You could not find a stable string or theme in their services.

I remember I noticed that one entrepreneur marketed to help people attract clients. Sometime later I saw his message to promote weight loss products, then after that something else.

Another entrepreneur tried to help women entrepreneurs find their feminine power. After a while, she started to work with school teachers on educational solutions, then new things again. Would you follow such "experts" to get help on solving your challenges or reaching your targets?

If you want to serve your clients the best, you would want to become an expert or master in your niche, and you would want your clients to believe in and treat you like an expert in your niche, only if you have a clear and sweet-spot business niche.

As we showed in Chapter 2 **the illustration of "Business Niche and Ideal Market"**, it's the central spot of these three overlaps: **Your Purposeful Passion, Your Gifts & Expertise, and the Market Needs and Segments.**

Would you believe that:

**When there is a purposeful passion, there is a market that needs it.**

In other words, if the market is not embracing your service, you may not be aligning with your purposeful passion yet.

Your purposeful passion, together with your gifts and expertise decide your value.

**Your niche is your best value needed by the ideal market.**

So make sure you find out your business niche that is aligned with your purposeful passion and can provide your best value to your ideal market.

## Top Mistake 3: Lack of System for Success

**Lack of Proven System with Abundant Wisdom, Accountable Process, Right Strategies, and Effective Tools**

When people pursue something, normally they do not have a clear plan and systematic ways to take action. We are easily distracted by daily duties and tasks. When we want to move from status A to status B, most of us bump into opportunities and follow them, then get lost in the middle somewhere.

Few of us has a proven system to refer to, that can guide us step by step to align our purpose and passions into life decisions, analyze situations and opportunities, make wise choices and decisions, set up right strategies, use effective tools, and make smart action plans that are practical and accountable.

Without such a proven system, you will have to make a lot more effort, go through a lot more trial and error, and take a much longer time to get to where you want to be if you are lucky.

Many people like to do New Year's resolutions. New Year's is a great time for people to review the past year, reflect on their progress or lessons, and envision a new chapter of their life.

According to some statistics, about 44% of Americans make *NEW YEAR'S RESOLUTIONS*. But for all these good intentions, only a tiny fraction of people keep their resolutions.

After one week since they make New Year's resolutions, 75% people still keep their resolutions. After one month, 64% keep theirs. By the 6th month, only 46% are still keeping their resolutions.

Research from the University of Scranton suggests that just **8% of people** achieve their New Year's goals.

The challenge for most people is how to make a SMART New Year's resolution that they can stick to and achieve. SMART means, Simple and Specific, Measurable and Tangible, Achievable, Realistic, and Time-bound. People need a great proven system to help them make such SMART resolutions and also hold them accountable through the journey with progress, achievement, and even setbacks that they will need strategies and tools to deal with so they can move forward.

Most solopreneurs are struggling in business operations, trading their personal time for money, and often feeling overwhelmed to cover every aspect of the business like a clumsy juggler. It's difficult to scale their business and sustain the development, because they don't understand how to build up and leverage an effective system for their success.

The next top mistake further explains why most people could not fulfill what they intend to.

## Top Mistake 4: Struggling By Yourself

**Without Powerful Support of Wisdom and Accountability, You May Give Up to Challenges and Inner Obstacles including Fears, Limiting Beliefs, Self Doubt and Procrastination**

You have been trying to figure things out all by yourself, struggling year after year, and blaming yourself for still not making it. During this process, you may hide in your shell or behind your desks, you may experience trials and failures, you may compare yourself with others feeling envious, unfair and frustrated. You need to walk out of **your safe shell and isolation**!

We human beings are not isolated creatures, but all connected intelligent learners and creators. Everyone needs help, and successful people become successful because they know how to get great help to transform themselves. The bigger ambitions, the greater wisdom and help you need, to gain better results, and deeper and longer impact.

As a result of self struggling, you could also have **lack of accountability**: No one is holding you accountable to set specific goals, take strategic actions, and create measurable results toward realizing your goals.

There are countless great **free resources**, but don't cheat yourself into thinking that you can find all the answers you need from only free resources designed generically for the public or for a certain group of people, and also for marketing and sales purposes. I am not denying the great benefits of many free educational and inspirational resources, actually we do need them, but we cannot rely only on them.

Honestly, this Abundant Train book is one of such great free to low-cost resources. It opens your views and insights, it inspires you with new information and perspectives, it intrigues you into new reflections, it recommends effective solutions, it empowers you to make courageous commitment and wise decisions, but it cannot answer all your specific life questions, to empower you and hold you accountable step by step from where you are now to where you want to be.

This book is a conscious knock and guidance for you to open the door to your passions, dream work and abundance.

Because of the lack of wise and effective ways and powerful support to deal with your fears, negative mindset and beliefs, self-doubt and procrastination, you could often get frustrated and eventually give up.

It's not because of your lack of commitment and perseverance. You have worked hard and tried your best. But without powerful support of wisdom and accountability, you are **vulnerable to outside challenges and your inner mental blocks**.

It is costly to go in a wrong direction, while giving up or shifting directions costs you more. Some may pass by their dreams forever. People give up most of their time not due to outside difficulties, but due to their own fears. When there is a lack of vision and results, and a lack of wise and effective ways to deal with their own fears, most people can easily give up.

Some people followed their passions, explored this and that, but eventually gave up due to having no financial rewards for a few years, which caused them to doubt themselves and believe that they can never succeed. What a huge pity and loss! **We lose the battle with ourselves!**

We need passions, commitment, strategies, actions, and also wisdom to break through challenges and hold on.

**Most failures could be avoided,** as long as people understand and actively seek great resources and create a supportive environment that can constantly provide inspirations, accountability and empowerment, which are all critical to your success.

In a normal and natural state, people would like to lay back and stay in their comfort zones. Without inspiring and empowering resources and environment, even great self-motivated people could often lose their momentum, take detours, prolong and even struggle through the journey to fulfill their desires.

**"If I have seen further, it is by *STANDING* upon the *SHOULDERS OF GIANTS.*" Sir Isaac *NEWTON*.**

Nowadays, most successful people have their coaches and mentors to provide different perspectives, empower them to stretch themselves, and hold them accountable to do what they plan to do and reveal their best potentials.

# 7. NEW MINDSETS FOR YOUR BREAKTHROUGHS

*"I am not a product of my circumstances. I am a product of my decisions."*

*~ Stephen Covey*

## Breakthrough Mindset 1:

## Believe that Abundance Is In Your Purpose and Birth Right

We are born to be happy and abundant, which is naturally and genetically encoded into our soul and heart. It's like our north star to which our inner compass will always point. Abundance guides every aspect of your life.

We human beings are all living on a purposeful journey, no matter if you realize it consciously or not. You will naturally desire a balance and abundance out of life, out of every relationship and out of every endeavor you are engaging in. Abundance is also your birth right, your most basic righteous need and also the most profound blessing for you to claim. Our heart and spirit are naturally connected to the purpose of abundance and are always yearning for it.

## Breakthrough Mindset 2:

## Your Abundance Needs Your Full Commitment to Claim

You can claim and achieve abundance, as long as you are fully conscious of it and commit to it. Commitment starts from clear awareness, then wise decisions, then consistent self discipline and devotion.

Commitment should be from the unity of your spirit, heart, mind and body. And the commitment should be at its fullest extent.

Abundance is a daily choice. From your mindset, to your attitude, to your strategies, to your actions, to your habits, you need the motivation to make the right choices aligned with abundance. Abundance is presence.

We mentioned "Follow your heart" before. When you follow your heart and commit to abundance, you can create abundance right away and enjoy it every day.

**Breakthrough Mindset 3:**

**Everyone Has Blind Spots**

When you stand within a situation, you normally cannot see the full picture, and you cannot always jump out of the box to think in different perspectives as well. You could also bear many limiting beliefs and unpleasant past experiences that can block you from exploring some new opportunities bravely and realizing your full potential.

You may have developed some negative habits that keep sabotaging yourself from revealing your best self and creating new milestones. There could be subconscious fears that are dragging you down and preventing you from moving forward.

These are the main reasons why many people get stuck in certain unsatisfied situations for many years, but could not get out or make breakthroughs by themselves.

You need to first see the situation from an outsider's eyes, and see things in different perspectives, before you can get the best inspirations and courage to jump out of a pit and make a difference, or further surpass the situation and even turn the challenge and difficulty into opportunity and success. This new mindset is to first humble your heart and empty yourself, before you can fill up with new wisdom and power.

**Breakthrough Mindset 4:**

**Succeed by Standing on the Shoulders of the Giant and the Great**

The people you hang around the most will decide your success. Choose friends and resources wisely.

Equip yourself with the secret weapon for success. Almost every successful person is a great learner. They learn from experts, masters, and leaders, and use professional coaches and mentors to help them make quicker and greater accomplishments. Some phenomenal executives and leaders even give such advice: Everyone needs a coach to succeed.

Using professional help is like standing on a giant's shoulders to explore the world so you can look farther and reach higher.

Even though sometimes you may want to quit or fail due to challenges and fears, your coach and mentor will hold you accountable and keep empowering your transformation and fulfillment.

## Breakthrough Mindset 5:

## Use Smart Systems to Accelerate the Process to Success

Nobody wants to waste their precious life and resources on unnecessary detours. Everyone wants to accelerate their process to success. No matter how smart you are, you need proven systems to save your time and money, and help you get to where you really want to be.

Smart systems will help you with practical wisdom and mindsets, right direction, accountable process, proven strategies, clear action plan and uplifting energy flow.

Smart systems will help hold you accountable and break down the journey into step-by step achievable tasks, so you can easily make progress and gain more confidence along the way.

Great systems will also train you with an abundant mindset and innovative method so you can create your best ways to effectively achieve your targets and fulfill more dreams.

# SECTION THREE:

# THE WISDOM AND NEW HORIZON

How I started to touch abundance is never an accident. I now understand this journey has been a mysterious guidance.

You read my resurrection story at the beginning. I was crushed, broken down, and ruined. I thought God must have forgotten me and abandoned me, for a long long time which felt dark and endless.

But before that, I had already started my journey to pursue the happiness purpose. I had become a life and business coach after closing my chapter of corporate experience. Maybe all the breaking down in the middle was rightly a purposeful preparation, a true test, from my dearest God.

In this section I will share more key stories, my epiphanies and transformations through this mysterious guidance, to help you understand the possible ways from the touch of abundance.

We'll then help you model Your Holistic Life leading to your Abundance.

Furthermore, we'll walk the shifting journey from Scarcity to Abundance, and learn the Secret Wisdom to Fulfill Your Purpose.

# 8. WELCOME TO THE HOME OF ABUNDANCE

*"Your life is most precious because you can*
*love, forgive, dream, learn, choose, create and serve."*
*~ Spring Zheng*

When I first arrived in the United States over 15 years ago from China, I already had 8 years of work experience with international companies and just graduated from a US prestigious Executive MBA program on International Finance and Business. I used over half a year to learn the local market especially New York City, and invested in improving myself for a new career.

I invested in my personal branding, resume, job searching and interview strategies, and key job resources in the US market, which eventually helped me land my director position in a Fortune 100 company's headquarters near Wall Street in Manhattan, managing performance and ecommerce projects across hundreds of international branches, with an annual income over 6 figures. That was 10 years ago.

After 5 years of being the director of international performance, as a direct impact of the 2008 global financial crisis, the Fortune 100 company and my department went through dramatic changes, including downsizing and relocation.

At that crossroad, instead of looking for another promising employer, I decided to leave the corporate world to search for my true purpose and passions, and what is really meaningful in life and work.

By that time, I had made quite a few successful career transitions, all followed my interests at those times, and my interests and explorations kept expanding.

From my first job as a Network Engineer at an international bank's headquarters, to operations administration in a well-known international IT corporation, to its sales and big account manager, then to its professional training management.

After that, I challenged and stretched myself into management consulting and strategic consulting crossing different industries: telecommunications, finance and IT industries, until I immigrated to the USA and started the performance and ecommerce projects management role at the Fortune 100 corporation.

Those explorations and adventures enriched my experiences and thoughts, and prepared me later for my discovery of my true purpose and passions.

In 2009, after I said goodbye to the corporate world, I took a few months to do profound reflection, study and research. This time instead of looking for external opportunities, I fully focused on connecting with myself, reflecting, understanding and revealing myself.

I also attended the Practical Philosophy School in Manhattan to further explore who I am and what I really want. I also utilized the career coaching service at Right Management which was planned for our job replacement.

As a result of the profound self-discovery process, and some training and guidance help from multiple career coaches, I defined my core values, and further clarified my life purpose.

From there, I did online research to match my purpose with a tangible career in this world. I finally settled on coaching, which was a totally new concept to me, but I already fell in love with it and believed right away that this was what I am called to do.

With the clear purpose and passion fuel, I decided quickly to reinvest in myself.

It was funny, as I thought that after EMBA my study life was over. On the contrary, since I chose coaching, my real life learning just started.

I studied and gained the professional coaching certificate from New York University, and extra specialized training and certificates from other cutting-edge coaching institutions. Since then I started to engage my whole heart and mind into abundance coaching practice to empower professionals, MBAs, entrepreneurs and business leaders to fulfill their purpose, passions and dreams.

One of my many innovative initiatives for coaching is, I used half a year to interview over 30 international professionals and entrepreneurs about their discoveries, breakthroughs and creations by following their passions. I then published the interview report **"Doing What You Love"** introducing their true stories and inspirations and my reflections based on the interviews. It has become a one-of-a-kind inspiration to people to courageously explore and fulfill their purpose and passions.

Today I continue to do Passion Interviews through *"NYC & Globe on Passions" project* and use live videos and my YouTube channel to bring even better and vivid inspirations to people.

After pursuing my purpose as a life and business coach, my personal life had a dramatic change as well.

I had a happy and confident childhood and teenager time, never really worried about school, career, relationships, or future, instead I was full of curiosity, dreams and passion.

After I grew up I experienced a lot of pain from my parents' divorce during my college freshman year, which deeply influenced my personal emotions and experience with love.

Then it's the love story I shared at the beginning of the book, how I was crushed, from heaven to hell, and eventually was guided into the world of abundance.

In my early adulthood, while in search of a whole family again after my parents' divorce and from the fear of losing love again, I lost myself in trying to pursue a perfect love, marriage and happiness. I struggled in emotional turmoil and even suicidal thoughts and behaviors for quite some years when I felt not fully cherished and loved by my husband who was my dearest first love with whom we went through over 10 years of long distance romance before marriage.

During our 13 years of partnership and marriage, I poured out all my soul, heart and youth to try to make the love and marriage wonderful, while he was not mature and his heart was not fully with me and the family. And we also found that a big gap formed from our different family values and paces of personal growth, especially after I started my journey as a life and business coach in which I had been on an accelerated learning and growth path compared to normal people.

Through 25 years of devotion and five years of struggling in my marital crisis, I've been learning to face the truth of who I really am and what spirit and values I could not sacrifice to compromise. I've been sharing the truth to my kids as well for their God-guided growth.

Going through all the pains, desperations and countless darkest nights, I gained guidance, wisdom, a new life and strength blessed from God. I finally broke through the cruelest trials and grew into abundance. As what I shared before, like a phoenix, resurrected through fire and ashes. I regained my life and freedom.

Living in truth and following God is part of who I am, even though it means to sacrifice many worldly benefits. **Telling and living the truth is a gracious and peaceful gift to oneself, and to others.**

I built up the Abundance system with all my learning and wisdom through the years to help others create their passionate business and abundant life, just like it healed and rebuilt me as well.

I am regaining myself like the child/teenager inside me, with new level of love, curiosity, confidence, joy and freedom. Abundance Coaching as my call and passion, is helping me access the abundance I have owned since the beginning!

Now when I celebrate my birthday, I reclaim my new life, freedom and abundance again! I thank God for the empowering abundance He has been recreating and blessing me with! It's like forever youth!

With my over 23 years of professional experience in both international corporations and coaching profession, plus a great synergy of Eastern ancient wisdom and Western practical philosophy, I have used many creative ways to thrive in both the corporate world and entrepreneur world.

As an immigrant getting into USA after my 30s with English as the second language, and then a mother of two kids, I have experienced many kinds of struggles, challenges, and pains.

With every trial and tribulation, I have learned how to overcome, appreciate and transform the obstacles, and eventually discovered the secrets to fulfill purpose and dreams effectively and efficiently.

I am so grateful that I have empowered many professionals, entrepreneurs and business leaders to make transformations and leaps that keep themselves wowed and proud. The Abundance world has become home to me, and now I'd welcome you to this abundance home as well.

**What are my BELIEFS as an Abundance Ambassador?**

•       My philosophy and belief as a thought leader and Abundance Ambassador is, to have an abundant life and successful business, we need first discover, align with and unleash our purpose, passions, gifts and inner wisdom, and fulfill our dreams through success strategies, system and consistent execution.

•       The Abundance System has helped me and my clients make phenomenal transformations in all aspects of our life, career and business. It will help you make breakthroughs on the most important life quests, that I call 5W's. This system will empower you to reveal your inner wisdom, do what you love strategically, and stand out confidently as an expert and leader to create your abundant life and business.

I will soon reveal the Abundance System in a full picture with details in the following chapters. So stay with me, you visionary creators!

## 9. Your Holistic Life to Abundance

"The future belongs to those who believe in the beauty of their dreams."

*~ Eleanor Roosevelt*

### Your Holistic Life Model

The Life Model concept has been popular in coaching and mentoring industry. Some may redesign and call it a Life Wheel. Some may adjust it to have fewer or more areas.

It generally addresses the main aspects of one's life and builds up a balanced model among them to express your needs in a holistic life.

Here below is an example of the Life Model with 7 major areas.

The key is the balance among all these aspects of your life. Many life coaches work on the balance to help you achieve a harmony or balance among these aspects of your life.

If we explore deeper, the core of your holistic life is actually your love, the love to yourself, the love to the world, and the love through your passionate work. To realize love at these levels are the deepest desires and dreams inside of us.

So if you focus on creating a purposeful and passionate career and business, that can fulfill your love and personal realization, boost your self-esteem and confidence, and bring your best values and gifts to the world, your other aspects like wellbeing, personal development, relationships, finance, etc. could all be fulfilled with ease and grace.

Which way is easier for you, working on all the 7 life aspects at the same time, or focusing on the core by creating your purposeful and passionate career and business in order to fulfill other aspects of life on an auto pilot? I believe you know the best answer.

### Your Abundance Warmup

As an Abundance and Thought Leadership Coach, I work with clients to not just achieve their balance between all the aspects of their life, but more profoundly, to fulfill their life's purpose and dreams by creating and developing their passion business with their gifts and purposeful niche, so their life can be fully uplifted to receive and give abundant blessings.

I normally have an Abundance Warmup exercise with my client at the beginning of our coaching.

We first explore **what abundance means to you.**

We then take an **assessment to find out your current abundance status stage,** as outlined below:

- Developing Stage
- Evolving Stage
- Balancing Stage
- Abundant Stage

Following that we have an **Abundance Breakthrough Exercise** to help you access the feeling of abundance right away.

After that, you are prepared to explore the full plate of Abundance!

If you are curious to learn and understand your current state on the abundance spectrum, feel free to contact us about a session on the abundance assessment and breakthrough exercise.

The next chapter will introduce you to the Abundance model.

# 10. SCARCITY TO ABUNDANCE, THE WISDOM TO FULFILL YOUR PURPOSE

*"You only live once, but if you do it right, once is enough."*

*~ Mae West*

Through years of exploration, studying and coaching practice, I have finally decoded the secret and the strongest power that can help people fulfill a greater life than they could originally imagine.

It looks simple, and it should be. But every essence of the power is so critical and aligned with each other, and each of them needs a life mastery to really conquer and use in the best way.

I developed the **"Abundant Happiness & Success on Purpose 5-Essence Model"**. Or simply, we call it **"The Abundance Model"**.

Based on the Abundance Model, I further discovered the strategic **Abundance System** that integrates all the major **Success Factors**, and is easily implemented to create measurable results.

# Abundant Happiness & Success on Purpose
# 5-Essence Model

In the Abundance Model, there are **5 Essences:**

**WHY, WHO, WHAT, HOW, WHEN**

Here below is the detailed illustration of these 5 Essences. Plus the explanations for each of the essences.

**WHY** — Your Purpose, Calling, Mission and Faith

**WHO** — Your Body, Mind, Heart and Spirit. Your 5-Step Wisdom Development

**WHAT** — Your Core Values, Dreams, Passions, Gifts, Vision, Money Power, Inner Voice

**HOW** — Your Mindset, Strategies, Tools, Action Plan, Environment, Energy Flow Practices

**WHEN** — Your Presence, Time Abundance, Happiness & Success Daily Habits, Fulfillment

**WHY:**

This is the biggest question of your life. Your Purpose, Calling, Mission, and Faith. This is what you are living for, and the meaning of your life.

**WHO:**

You are a unique unity of your body, mind, heart and spirit. This is your true BEING, that no one else could replace. Your wisdom is already born with your being, waiting for you to discover the treasure and grow your asset.

**WHAT:**

You bring with your life a unique combination of treasures and blessings, including your core values, dreams, passions, gifts, visions, sacred money power, and inner voice or intuition.

**HOW:**

All these components will decide your success and determine whether you can fulfill your purpose and passions: your mindset, habits, energy, environment, niche strategies, and actions.

**WHEN:**

Your journey's milestones and time-bounded targets, time abundance, smart calendar planning, happiness and success building daily habits, and your presence. All these are time related. Do the Right Things at the Right Time.

The **Abundance System**, including the Abundance Model, its step-by-step guidance, exercises, and coaching will help you develop the **5 Essence Powers** within yourself as the synergic foundation to create your dream business, to fulfill your best purpose using your passions and gifts, and live an abundant life in happiness and success.

Now it's the time to reveal the big picture of what **Success FACTORS** you need specifically to fulfill your business success and life abundance. Here is a quick peek of the success factors:

**Abundance Wisdom (with Purposeful Passion) +**

**Abundance Mindset +**

**Success Habits +**

**Positive Energy +**

**Supportive Environment +**

**Niche Strategies +**

**Accountable Actions**

**=> Happiness & Success!**

The Abundance System will help you achieve many levels of discoveries and realizations, from spirituality, thought leadership, emotional health to practical results, including the **4P's Realization.**

# 4P's Realization

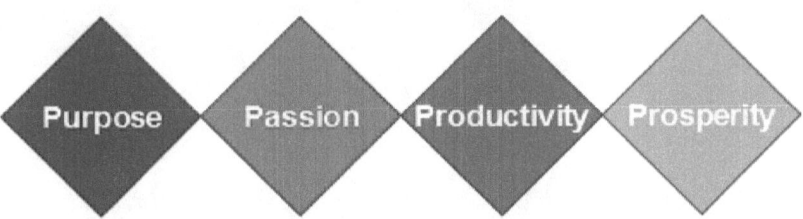

The Abundance System can help you go deeper and also stretch you to expand. It helps you overcome your fears and solve your challenges. This system can help you step by step to reveal your life's true meaning, clarify your passions and dreams, develop a holistic lifestyle, build up a strong foundation for you to do what you love and create your dream business, and start to live a purposeful, fulfilling, happy and successful life.

Here below is an illustration of **the Abundance System with the major Business Success Factors.**

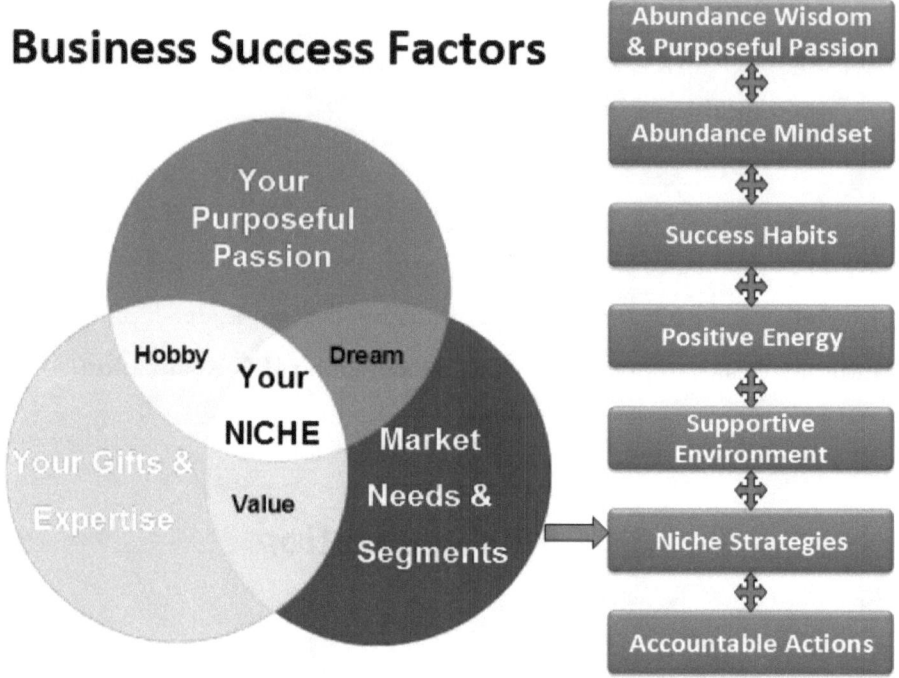

Now you may get these questions, what are the main strategies and principles in this system and these success factors, and how to easily implement them?

Yes, that's the mission of the following two sections. Let's get into the system to see how to apply it in practice and turn abundance into measurable results.

# SECTION FOUR:

# THE SECRET STRATEGIES AND SYSTEM

Now after working on our inner battles, our mindset, and our wisdom shift, let's get on the strategic practice to build our system in the market that could help us fulfill our abundance from inside to outside.

Every leader and great impact needs a strategic and efficient system for support. Every entrepreneur is a creator. In this section we'll decode Abundance. And we'd call the Abundance manifestation and strategic system as the Abundance Code, which has both the wisdom and the creation.

The Abundance Code is never a static thing, nor an invisible thing. It manifests through the system we build that connects us with the market and our ideal clients, and it expresses itself through the values we generate for the people and the world.

We will learn how to use the Abundance Code to CREATE Your Lucrative Business and Meaningful Impact.

Within the Abundance Code System, we'll further explain the important success foundation for any business, to clarify your Purposeful and Profitable Niche. Then explain how to build your Visibility Secrets system to spread your messages to the market and attract your right audience and dream clients to you, instead of chasing after someone in the open market.

This section shares the secrets for you to do things differently, uniquely, and aligned with your purpose and passion, so that you can stand out as an expert and leader to transform and impact more lives.

# 11. THE ABUNDANCE CODE TO CREATE YOUR BUSINESS AND IMPACT

*"What you love and God's will for you are one and the same......*
*When you are passionate, failure is not an option."*
*~ Janet and Chris Attwood.*

The Abundance Code System can help people achieve Abundant Happiness and Success on Purpose. No matter what you have experienced or achieved before, no matter what life stage you are in now, and no matter what specific targets you are pursuing, the Abundance Code System can empower you with new perspectives and wisdom to open a new and greater chapter of your life.

Through my coaching practice with visionary entrepreneurs, life changers (such as coaches, authors, speakers, and consultants), business owners, professionals, MBAs, and business leaders, using the core of the Abundance Code System, I developed the 7-Step Formula, to help you discover, design, attract, create, launch / re-launch your passion business and at the same time to live a meaningful and prosperous life.

"The Abundance Code: Unleash Your Purpose and Passion to CREATE a Lucrative Business and Meaningful Impact in the World!"

### THE SOLUTION – I C.R.E.A.T.E.!

The Abundance Code System will empower you to take 7 critical steps to make profound transformations and C.R.E.A.T.E. abundance in both your life and business!

1.  **I: Discover Your Big WHY and Embrace WHO You Are**

2.  **Clarity: Reveal WHAT Treasures You Own to Ignite Your Vision and Blueprint**

3.  **Relationships: Build up Meaningful Connections for Positive Environment and Opportunities**

4.  **Energy: Develop Abundance Mindset, Build Success Habits, and Master Your Energy**

5.  **Asset: Your Business System - Define Your Purposeful and Profitable Niche, Design Your Unique Branding, Develop Your Irresistible Offer, Create Your Attractive Content, Publish Your Signature Speaking and Theme Shows, and Grow Your Secret Garden - Your Tribe and Community**

**6. Touch: Launch / Re-Launch Your Passion Business to Touch the Ideal Market**

**7. Expansion: Attract More Ideal Clients and Monetize Your Passion Business**

Here below are details of the **Outcomes** each step will help you achieve.

**STEP 1. I: Discover Your Big WHY and Embrace WHO You Are**

• Understand the Common Purpose and discover your specific CALLING and WHY
• Make your Mission Statement and start to live on your Purpose Now
• Understand WHO you are: your unique unity of body, mind, heart and spirit
• Discover your identity, birth rights and hallmark
• Develop your 5 essential self-knowledge wisdom
• Connect with your wisdom sources, increase your consciousness, self love and confidence to reach your greatest potential

**STEP 2. Clarity: WHAT Treasures You Own to Ignite Your Vision**

• Reveal and clarify your passions, talents, core values, dreams, visions and intuition.
• Alignment with your inner gifts and treasures.
• Develop your Creative Vision Board.
• Make a SMART Action Plan according to your vision board.

**STEP 3. Relationships: Build Up Meaningful Connections for Positive Environment and Opportunities**

• Analyze your current environment, what's working and what's not serving your purpose.

• Define your ideal environment focusing on people network.

• Strategies to build up your heart-centered, positive and supportive environment.

• Create and grasp opportunities that serve your purpose and passion the best.

**STEP 4. Energy: Develop Abundant Mindset, Build Success Habits, and Master Your Energy**

• Learn 7 abundance attitudes and develop your abundance mindset.

• Take accountable and effective actions.

• Develop 9 success habits to increase your presence, balance, focus, prioritization, productivity and quality of life.

• Learn Abundance Everyday 11 Magic Energy Practices.

• Trace your energy flow and build up your best energy practice, master your energy to be unstoppable and manifest anything you want.

**STEP 5. Asset: Your Business System - Define Your Purposeful and Profitable Niche, Design Your Unique Branding, Develop Your Irresistible Offer, Create Your Attractive Content, Publish Your Signature Speaking and Theme Shows, and Grow Your Secret Garden - Your Tribe and Community**

- Clarify your big idea, define your business niche and ideal clients.
- Design your unique personal and business branding system.
- Develop your signature program and irresistible offer.
- Create your strategic and attractive content that resonate with your ideal audience.
- Develop your signature talk and theme shows to convey core marketing messages.
- Grow your secret garden and enable your community to thrive as a confident leader.

We put these key business asset components into a system and will discuss more in the next chapter of *Your Visibility Secrets*.

**STEP 6. Touch: Launch / Re-launch Your Passion Business to Touch the Ideal Market**

- Develop a strategic implementation plan for launch.
- Set up your fundamental marketing and sales system and process.
- Design and build your ideal marketing funnels.
- Launch your passion business with innovative product and program.
- Turn your signature program evergreen.

**STEP 7. Expansion: Attract More Ideal Clients and Monetize Your Passion Business**

• Develop your heart-centered networking, marketing, and social media strategies.

• Nurture your leads list and build up influence and loyalty with your expertise.

• Master the Law of Attraction to magnify your ideal clients and prosperity.

• Apply the best Joint Venture (JV) strategies to help multiply your market presence and convert more ideal clients quickly.

We have both 90-Day Accelerated Program and Annual Academy on the Abundance Code Coaching System. Contact us to consult and apply for the right program for your best development.

# 12. YOUR PURPOSEFUL AND PROFITABLE NICHE

*"Obsessively specialize. No niche is too small if it's yours."*
*~ Seth Godin*

Here is a special story of my epiphany experiences during the 10 years of coaching practice and business exploration.

First I'd like to share with you my deep desires.

I want to become a successful coach by helping a lot of clients, creating a fulfilling life and business, and making global impact.

I want to have a happy family, better life quality, with more quality time together.

I wanted to be recognized by my family, my friends and my kids as a successful and very valuable person to match my previous honorable records. I want to leave a noble legacy.

I shared earlier that a few years ago, my life was dramatically flipped and turned upside down. It was totally out of the blue, me and my husband experienced a severe marriage and trust crisis and almost got divorced. My heart was broken and I lost my hope to go on. It was like an endless dark tunnel from which I could never walk out. I tried to end the pains by ending my life...

Where I thought would be the end of my life story…by a miracle, I was saved, thanks to God's grace and mercy. I realized that God must have some unfinished plan with my life.

I have been praying that God would guide me through my purpose, passion and coaching practice to serve more people and fulfill greater meanings.

During my darkest years, one thing I did right was that I grasped a light. The light was in continuous self-development and growth, with even more focus and investment.

I saw many successful experts and masters in the industry doing what they love. I wondered, why could they achieve success, but the majority of others could not? I decided to learn more deeply from them and decode the success secrets.

So I started to re-invest in myself, personal growth, learning from industrial experts and masters.

Through close observation and personally experiencing those mentors teaching, I discovered the secrets and the Abundance Model that most experts and masters have used in different ways to reach their success in the market. I started to adapt the Abundance Model into my coaching and grew from a Happiness Coach into Abundance Coach.

Referring to the Abundance Model, I reviewed my existing coaching practice, discarded what did not work for me anymore, and re-innovated my whole new system. I developed new coaching programs and webinar presentations, started to serve some private clients, and started to build up my community.

After a few years of exploration and practice, I found that I tried to help everyone who got in touch with me, and I gave away too much for free. My marketing messages and campaigns were not converting enough clients, even though I was super passionate and providing great inspirations. My coaching was still not a real business that generated a good profit.

And there were many other passionate entrepreneurs just like me, our passions did not pay off. Though we were glad that we were doing what we love, but because we were not good at marketing and sales, it's not rewarding financially.

That's painful, and unfulfilling!

My passion, energy and self-worth were severely challenged. I started to get frustrated even though I was still passionate about what I was doing. I started to doubt myself and the direction I chose.

And I needed to contribute money and value to my family as well, especially for my two little kids who were becoming teenagers with more desires and questions about life, dreams, personal growth, and their future.

I desired to be a successful role model for them, by figuring out how to turn my passion and dream into reality, instead of following the normal standards and ladders set up by the society that has created millions of suffering employees.

I wanted to show my kids and my clients a way of abundance and freedom with personal dedication and smart business engagement.

I decided to further learn how other successful experts and masters are doing and practicing in the market, what are their deeper secrets.

So I invested more in my personal, business and system development, and I've been continuously investing in myself and my coaching business since then, to learn from the best of the best in the market, from coaching, mentoring, live events, mastermind programs, webinars, public speaking events, to align my genius with my right offers and my right market.

I learned how to further clarify my gifts and my niche, crushed many false beliefs, and strengthened my mindset, branding, message, content and presence with abundance coaching in the market.

The best secrets I learned and practiced started to make breakthroughs in my business:

- I started to believe that good marketing and sales are the best ways to spread valuable messages and serve people's needs,

- I started to attract more of the right audiences and clients,

- I started to charge higher fees with more confidence,

- I started to speak in public with resonating and powerful messages,

- I started to have renewing clients, again and again, and

- I started to develop a thriving community with thousands of visionary entrepreneur members.

I've been engaging with more of my ideal audience and dream clients every day, feeling more than ever aligned, confident and fulfilling.

All these positive changes and results started because I discovered, defined and clarified my ideal niche that matches with my purpose, my genius, and my most loved market, and I started to claim my ideal niche as an owner and to present every day consistently in the marketplace with my powerful niche messages!

I know that many entrepreneurs are still struggling with how to find their ideal market, sweet zone, powerful messages, irresistible offer and impactful presence.

The lack of clarity of their niche has cost them to lose great opportunities in the market, and suffering from little results and rewards compared to their big passion and giving.

Over 90% of startups fail every year because their products and services were not needed by the market, which is mainly because they don't understand what their right market is and what are the best messages and offers that their ideal clients would resonate with and respond to.

I decided to put all the secrets and best practice I have learned through the years into **coaching programs**, to end the struggling of most entrepreneurs, save them years of trial and error, help them discover their best niche market and ideal clients, design the right offer, messages and content, and make the greatest impact and results in the marketplace!

So on the basis of ***the Abundance Model*** which builds up a powerful and unstoppable mindset, and with the guidance of ***the Abundance Success Factors System*** introduced in the last chapter, I developed the **Purposeful and Profitable Niche Secrets Program**, to help entrepreneurs claim their ideal niche, and design irresistible messages and offer to attract their dream clients.

The Purposeful and Profitable Niche Secrets program helps visionary entrepreneurs use 4 simple steps to transform their passion and genius into an abundant niche business.

Through 5 weeks of live coaching, you will experience the 4 signature **"WING"** modules and benefits, which is like helping you grow new wings so that you could fly.

### *Module #1: Reveal Your Big "Why"*

1.1 Why Niche, and Why Niche on Purpose

1.2 Introduce the 3-Key Niche Clarity Model

1.3 Discover Your Life's Purpose

1.4 Make Your Ultimate Mission Statement

### *Module #2: Unleash Your Unique "Identity"*

2.1 Discover WHO You Truly Are and Why You Are Special

2.2 Uncover Your Passion, Dream, Vision and Core Values

2.3 Reveal Your Unique Gifts and Talents

2.4 Polish Your Best Credibility and Expertise

### *Module #3: Discover Your Ideal Market "Nature"*

3.1 Who Do You Love to Help and Serve

3.2 Your Dream Client Profile

3.3 Where to Find Your Dream Clients

3.4 What Are They Eagerly Looking For

### *Module #4: Claim Your Niche "Greatness"*

4.1 Generate Your Big Idea and Solution

4.2 Clarify Your Ideal Market and Benefits

4.3 Match Your Ideal Market and Solution with Your Identity

4.4 Claim Your Great Purposeful and Profitable Niche

Through the Purposeful and Profitable Niche Secrets program, you will claim your purposeful and profitable niche with one hundred percent clarity.

You will keep attracting your ideal audience and dream clients even during your sleep.

You will be able to charge higher fees with confidence.

You will be speaking in public with your niche message that resonates and sells.

You will be able to develop a thriving community with your ideal members.

You will be engaging with more of your dream clients, feeling aligned, joyful and fulfilled every day.

You could have all this without wasting time, money and energy anymore!

You may visit https://coaching.springmagiclife.com/nichesecrets to learn more about the Purposeful and Profitable Niche Secrets Program.

Claim your ideal niche first to own your abundant business!

## 13. YOUR VISIBILITY SECRETS

*"Try not to be a man of success. Rather become a man of value."*
*~ Albert Einstein*

When you finally own your purposeful and profitable niche, what is the next step in developing your abundant business?

You've got a great purpose to fulfil, an ideal market to serve, a great message to share, you cannot wait!

At the same time, you may feel anxious, nervous or even fearful to spread your message and provide your offer. Or you may feel overwhelmed by the busy, competitive and noisy market, and don't know where to start. Isn't it true?

Everything now depends on how confident you are, and how you show up in the market.

Based on all my observations and learnings from those successful masters, and my years of trial and error followed by best practice, I know how critical it is to PRESENT RIGHT in the market. If you cannot present right, no matter how great your messages or offers are, you cannot win the clients and generate the impact you want.

So I developed the **Visibility Secrets Program**, to help visionary entrepreneurs and life changers learn how to step up and stand out in the market as confident experts and thought leaders in their ideal niche with their unique gifts to transform more lives, and positively impact the world for the abundance of all.

Here is an overview of the major modules and benefits of the Visibility Secrets Program:

## MODULE #1:
## STEP INTO YOUR EXPERT POWER AND SUCCESS WITH CONFIDENCE

> Success is an Iceberg. Build Success into Your Mindset and Reality

> Claim Your Greatest Niche Following Your Heart and Strength

> Define Your Clear Vision, Business Blueprint and 90-Day Road Map

> Optimize Your Core Solution to Solve Real Problems

> Meet Your Ideal Audience Where They Are Meant to Be

*Results and Benefits of Module 1:*

You will claim your crystal clear niche, own your clear long-term vision, short-term goals and strategic action plan, package your core solution and hot offer, and be fully confident in your mindset and service to present to your ideal audience and clients.

## MODULE #2:

## POSITION YOUR EXPERT PERSONAL AND BUSINESS BRANDING

> Your Expert Title, Pitches, and Bio

> Your Expert Social Media Profiles

> Your Business Name, Intro and Website

> Your Social Media Business Fan Page

*Results and Benefits of Module 2:*

You will own your powerful branding both personally and professionally that are fully aligned with your ideal niche, and all your branding will be consistent throughout your social media profiles and personal presence.

## MODULE #3:

## PLAY YOUR MAGIC POKER (STRATEGIC AND CREATIVE CONTENT)

> Prepare Your Signature Messages, Stories and Movement

> Design Your Magic Poker Content: Visuals, Stories and Videos

> Use Advanced Content Creator Effectively

> Make Your Consistent Expert Presence as an Inspiring Leader

*Results and Benefits of Module 3:*

You will become an expert in creating your strategic and attractive content that conveys your passion and talents, and presenting confidently in the market. And you will start to attract a larger audience that is right for you and clients who are interested in learning more from you.

## MODULE #4:
## HOST YOUR SIGNATURE EXPERT THEME SHOWS (FACEBOOK LIVE, YOUTUBE, PUBLIC SPEAKING)

> Generate Intriguing Ideas and Hot Topics on Your Expertise

> Create Your Signature Expert Theme Shows

> Master Abundant Expert Content Creator for Strategic and Attractive Topics

> Present Consistently to Your Signature Shows that Attract and Convert

*Results and Benefits of Module 4:*

You will design and launch your theme shows, become expert in initiating new strategic topics, speak more confidently to your right audience and clients, and make the right call to action to your offers.

## MODULE #5:
## PLANT YOUR SECRET GARDEN – YOUR OWN THRIVING GROUP (LEADERSHIP & COMMUNITY)

> Choose a Great Group Name Matching your Niche and Brand

> Define Clear Group Purpose, Description, Rules and Themes

> Invite, Attract and Sustain Your Ideal Audience to Help the Community Thrive

> Put All Your Social Media Presence in Powerful Alignment

*Results and Benefits of Module 5:*

You will design and launch your online community, invite the right people to join, host it with a great vision and leadership, master the strategies on how to engage and help your group thrive, and monetize from your inner circle community.

**A summary review on the whole Abundance Code System and programs:**

The Purposeful and Profitable Niche Secrets Program and the Visibility Secrets Program are both available as stand-alone programs to meet visionary entrepreneurs' needs at different development stages.

For those entrepreneurs and life changers who need comprehensive abundance coaching support, we integrate these four critical components together: Abundance Model, Abundance Success Factors System, Purposeful and Profitable Niche Secrets, and Visibility Secrets, for the one holistic and strategic masterpiece system: **ABUNDANCE CODE SYSTEM**, on which we introduced the major I CREATE modules in chapter 11.

The Abundance Code System applies abundance in both life and business, in both entrepreneurship and thought leadership, covering levels from mindset to energy to strategy to accountable action and implementation.

Using the Abundance Code System, I have tripled my leads and income, and grown my niche tribe to serve thousands of abundant entrepreneurs. I also helped my clients through the abundance code coaching to lead their life, business and communities with more confidence and financial results.

Through the Abundance Code System, I'm now living out my purpose every day loving and believing in myself, enjoying more of what I do as an abundant entrepreneurship and thought leadership coach, and having ownership of my life, emotions, and business opportunities to reach my higher potential.

I'm also spending more quality time with my family and kids, building role model for my kids, and having better ways to inspire and cultivate their growth.

The Abundance Code System is the game changer, and the backbone of my coaching business, which enabled me and my clients to live, attract and impact consciously in abundance every day.

You are welcome to contact us for a complimentary consultation on the Abundance Code System. We have both Accelerated Coaching program and Annual Academy on this system to meet your specific needs.

# SECTION FIVE:

# YOUR ACTION AND IMPACT

No matter what great wisdom and strategies you learn, no matter which great coaches and mentors you learn from, what matters the most is your commitment and action.

This section is your time to apply what you have learned and implement it into practice, into your business. It's also test time, to make sure what you have learned could really work in your life and business.

Don't wait days and weeks after you finish learning to take action. By then you may have forgotten what you have learned. Tony Robbins always emphasizes to his students and followers that we should take immediate action, so what we learn could immediately turn into practice and something valuable in our life or business, some reality, instead of just knowledge. He knows what human nature is, and that the majority of us would just stay in our comfort zone if not urged to take immediate action.

Strategies are nothing unless they work for you. We tend to forget easily, not take action, find excuses, procrastinate, regret, hate, become frustrated, and then give up. So it's now, or never.

That's why some experts say, we should always take inspired action. While you are inspired and motivated, take action, that's the best time we commit and make changes really happen. Then we get a good start and further motivation to take the next steps.

If such momentum continues, we could get into a positive movement and make some really meaningful and valuable changes. That's the secret to make knowledge become useful practice and turn it into reality.

# 14. ACTION NOW TO START YOUR ABUNDANCE TODAY

*"The future depends on what you do today."*
*~ Mahatma Gandhi*

Tony Robbins shared his secret on how you can change your life in a moment. He said, take a deep breath and remind yourself – "I'm gonna live in a beautiful state no matter what!"

That's a great declaration. Tony encouraged people to practice appreciation.

"Could you find something in this moment to feel joyous about, to appreciate, to feel ecstatic about if you really want to? Yes or No?"

"Trade your expectations for appreciation, your whole life will change in that moment. 'Cause the minute we appreciate things, all the sufferings are gone."

I love Tony's teaching and inspirations. I believe most times this appreciation method works.

Occasionally, I wound find myself in some very challenging and discouraging moments when I could not immediately use my appreciation muscles, that my emotions were so low that I felt paralyzed, and my brain would not like to try appreciation even though I knew it could work. Then what eventually worked for me?

When my inside energy and power was not enough to lift myself up, I connected myself with the higher wisdom and intelligence, my God.

I told myself that I could waste this moment or today in such miserable state, and this time as a unique part of my life will never come back again. I will lose it in such a negative state. A waste of my life. And I reminded myself that my God is always with me, and He has all the abundant blessings for me already, so much that I have not seen most of them with my limited human eyes.

Faith, more than any appreciation, always saves me, even from the most miserable states. And it's something I can always trust.

Throughout the past 10 years and more, I have put enormous passion, time, investment and energy to practice and develop the Abundance Code System with 7-Step Formula for visionary entrepreneurs, life changers and business owners. I am dedicated to empowering them and holding them accountable to take step-by-step actions toward living a purposeful, successful and fulfilling life, and furthermore, standing out as experts and thought leaders to impact the world.

**The main Transformations I have empowered my clients to make:**

▶ Unleash their purpose, passions and gifts to do what they love, claim their purposeful and profitable niche, and strategically monetize their niche business.

▶ Take better control of their lives with abundant wisdom, confidence, energy and thought leadership.

▶ Create special movement with their meaningful missions, happiness, freedom, wealth and impact to transform many other lives, and fulfill the abundance of all.

You may like to hear what my clients say about the abundance coaching services they have received. Check our website: http://www.springmagiclife.com/testimonials/.

I created this Abundant Train book with my best knowledge and practice for you to leap to the next level of your consciousness, and open your horizon to access your abundance. I really thank you for reading this book up until this point. I fully appreciate your curiosity, ambitions, and ownership for your best destiny. Now, it is your turn to take actions to make your dream come true.

If you strongly resonate with the Abundance Code System to create your lucrative business and meaningful impact in the world, you may wish to learn more about it and how this system could help you fulfill your dreams.

I have **Two Exciting GIFTS** for you!

## GIFT 1

**Webinar:**

**"How to Attract Your Dream Clients and Impact the World, Even If You Just Started Entrepreneurship or Have Already Tried Everything"**

This webinar will greatly **benefit** you by **revealing in more details on**:

* How to avoid the most common mistakes and #1 business killer
* How to discover and claim your ideal niche business
* How to be seen as an expert and leader in the market for greater attraction and results
* Answers to your questions and much more

Sign up to our eNewsletter for Abundant Entrepreneurs to receive inspirations and resources including the free webinar invitation:

https://springabundancecoaching.clickfunnels.com/websitesignup

## GIFT 2

## Complimentary One-on-One
## "Abundant Business Breakthrough Session"

Occasionally I give complimentary one-on-one "Abundant Business Breakthrough Session" to highly passionate and committed entrepreneurs and life changers, who desire to create their purposeful and prosperous business, and fulfill an abundant life. There is no obligation to any part of the complimentary 45-minute coaching session. You purely get great value for free!

Inside this complimentary "Abundant Business Breakthrough Session", you will:

* Clarify a crystal clear VISION and GOALS of your dream life and business;

* Uncover the hidden OBSTACLES that are sabotaging your ability to attract more ideal clients, more money, and more abundance;

* Create a simple step-by-step ACTION PLAN to close the gap, and invite abundance into your life and business right away, and leave the session renewed, re-energized and fully ready to create your dream life and impactful business!

To become one of the lucky people for the highly-valued complimentary breakthrough session, please contact us at: i@SpringMagicLife.com.

**Email Subject: Abundant Business Breakthrough Session**

Please include in the email: your Full Name, Email Address, and a brief Self Introduction.

Then you may be asked a few simple questions for the application.

After you submit your email application, we'll notify you within three days if you were accepted for a breakthrough session. If you are approved, you will be given a link to book your appointment at your preferred date and time. We will use Zoom video conference for the one-on-one session.

You can achieve clarity and breakthrough soon by taking this simple action.

## 15. TAKE CHALLENGE AS YOUR BEST FRIENDS
## TO CREATE ABUNDANCE TOGETHER

"Every dream and passion has a great destiny blessed by God, and your duty as its owner is to carry it on and commit to its realization."

~ *Spring Zheng*

Just like life will never be perfect, the world will never be short of challenges.

Instead of giving abundance a definition at the beginning of the book like many other books may do, I'm offering a clearer definition of Abundance at the end of the book, after we have shared and discussed the major content, and also given your thinking and imagination free space to stretch and expand.

Online various dictionaries provide these definitions for Abundance:
- A very large quantity of something.
- An ample quantity.
- An extremely plentiful or over sufficient quantity or supply.
- Affluence, wealth a life of abundance.

- Abundance is the opposite of scarcity. An abundance of wealth is a ton of cash.

- An amount that is more than enough.

- The situation in which there is more than enough of something.

These definitions mainly focus on quantity or amount. I'd add two more layers of definition to Abundance, to include our human selves as the core subject, one is on the quality and meaningfulness, another is on aspects and dimensions.

To me,

Abundance is living your true self and living your blessed faith, purpose, passions and gifts;

Abundance is loving yourself, doing what you love, and loving all by giving your gifts to serve, and as a result;

Abundance is having more than enough and unlimited joy, prosperity and freedom on every aspect of your life;

Abundance is the purpose, and the fulfillment.

Many people may not fully understand the difference between abundance and happiness.

I used to think happiness is our common purpose, till I personally experienced my life's crushing down and resurrection.

I understood that even when one may lose happiness temporarily and suffer inside heavily, one could still live in a peaceful and tranquility state with resilience, forgetting about self and engaging into the greatness of serving others, a state very close to abundance.

I remember I discovered a trinity wisdom formula for lasting happiness before, which I found is actually more suitable for lasting abundance. We may simplify life into 3 core areas and the wisdom formula for abundance is:

- Wellbeing Wisdom – Love Yourself Abundantly

- Career & Wealth Wisdom - Do What You Love Strategically

- Relationship Wisdom – Love All Unconditionally

In all these three areas we could meet continuous challenges as well. It's like a dance. One side we pursue abundance, another side we deal with challenges. Abundance and challenges (or even adversities) are like dancing partners who could not perform alone but together create some wonderful and magical dances.

So if you want to achieve abundance, you should invite challenges. Don't wait for or avoid challenges. Instead, you want to take proactive actions, to welcome challenges, and even create challenges so that you can create abundance as well. Abundance, most often, is like a wonderful and beautiful scenery at the end of the storm, which is the challenge.

Much of my best progress and results were achieved when I was taking challenges. Some are from my mentors and coaches, most are created by myself. Like my 30-day One Funnel Away Challenge, 7-day Product Launch challenge, Passion Interview challenge, 5-day Vision challenge, 365 days Abundance Today challenge, Niche decoding challenge, Facebook Live daily challenge, Book writing and publishing challenge, License Exam challenge, Leads challenge, JV partners challenge, etc.

I've taken numerous challenges through my coaching business practice. Every time I completed them, I also increased confidence and faith in myself, and much more.

When my clients work with me, they are encouraged, inspired, empowered, and also challenged.

Through all my coaching and my programs, you could see step by step wisdom, strategies, execution, and also challenges, and accountabilities.

Regardless of whether it is Purposeful and Profitable Niche Secrets, or Visibility Secrets, or the whole Abundance Code System, guided challenges are there to stretch and expand you along the way, until you reach the next level. I believe challenges are the best tools to help you grow and accelerate your business development.

I encourage you to start loving challenges, no matter how uncomfortable you may feel at the beginning. Step out of your box, your comfort zone, seek challenges, and be excited for them! That's where your life and business could experience the biggest breakthroughs and make the fastest transformations.

Take challenges as your best friends to create Abundance together!

Be a visionary, brave and confident Abundance Creator starting today!

### The Ending of this Book, the New Start of Your Life

*Your life is most precious because you can love, forgive, dream, learn, choose, create, and serve.*

*Following your passion and doing what you love is a blessed job from God. Hold the faith that you can never fail on this divine journey.*

Let's work together to make your dreams come true!

I look forward to getting to know you personally and empowering you to master your Abundance Code and to create your lucrative business on purpose, and an abundant life with unlimited love, wisdom, happiness, success and impact!

Thank you, and here is to your abundant life and business!

*Spring Zheng*

Abundant Entrepreneurship & Thought Leadership Coach
Empowering Visionary Entrepreneurs & Life Changers to Stand Out in the Market as Experts and Leaders!
Founder of Spring Magic Life Society, Inc.
www.SpringMagicLife.com
**Email:** i@SpringMagicLife.com
**Facebook Fan Page:** Spring Zheng – Live, Serve, Fulfill.
**Facebook Group:** Abundant Entrepreneurs
**Instagram:** @SpringZhengAbundance
**YouTube Channel:** https://www.youtube.com/user/SpringMagicLife
**LinkedIn:** Spring Zheng
**Twitter:** @SpringMagicLife
**Inspirations / Blog:** http://springmagiclife.wordpress.com/
Spring Link Tree: https://linktr.ee/springzhengabundance
Spring's Motto: Love never fails. Live in faith, passion and abundance.

# 7 SIMPLE STEPS:
# YOUR CHECKLIST FOR ABUNDANCE
# IN BOTH LIFE AND BUSINESS

## STEP 1. I: Discover Your Big WHY and Embrace WHO You Are

1.  Do you understand the Common Purpose and have discovered your specific CALLING and WHY?

2.  Have you made your Mission Statement and started to live on your Purpose every day?

3.  Do you understand WHO you are? Are you clear about your unique unity of body, mind, heart and spirit, and your specialty in each part?

4.  Have you discovered your identity, birth rights and hallmark?

5.  Have you developed your 5 essential self-knowledge wisdom?

6.  Are you clear about and connecting with your wisdom sources? Do you know how to increase your consciousness, self love and confidence to reach your greatest potential?

## STEP 2. Clarity: WHAT Treasures You Own to Ignite Your Vision

1.  Have you revealed and clarified your passions, talents, core values, dreams, visions and intuition?

2.  Are you in alignment with your inner gifts and treasures?

3.  Have you developed your Creative Vision Board?

4.  Have you made a SMART Action Plan according to your vision board?

## STEP 3. Relationships: Build Up Meaningful Connections for Positive Environment and Opportunities

1.  Have you analyzed your current environment, what's working and what's not serving your purpose?
2.  Have you defined your ideal environment focusing on people network?
3.  What effective strategies can you learn to build up your heart-centered, positive and supportive environment?
4.  Do you know the criteria and how to create and grasp opportunities that serve your purpose and passion the best?

## STEP 4. Energy: Develop Abundant Mindset, Build Success Habits, and Master Your Energy

1.  Do you know the 7 abundance attitudes and have you developed your abundance mindset?
2.  Are you taking accountable and effective actions every day?
3.  Have you developed 9 success habits to increase your presence, balance, focus, prioritization, productivity and quality of life?
4.  Have you learned Abundance Everyday 11 Magic Energy Practices?
5.  Have you traced your energy flow and built up your best energy practice? Do you know the most effective ways to master your energy to be unstoppable and manifest anything you want?

**STEP 5. Asset: Your Business System - Define Your Purposeful and Profitable Niche, Design Your Unique Branding, Develop Your Irresistible Offer, Create Your Attractive Content, Publish Your Signature Speaking and Theme Shows, and Grow Your Secret Garden - Your Tribe and Community**

1.  Have you clarified your big idea, define your business niche and ideal clients?

2.  Have you designed your unique personal and business branding system?

3.  Have you developed your signature program and irresistible offer?

4.  Are you creating your strategic and attractive content that resonate with your ideal audience?

5.  Have you developed your signature talk and theme shows platform to convey core marketing messages?

6.  Are you growing your secret garden and enabling your community to thrive as a confident leader?

**STEP 6. Touch: Launch / Re-launch Your Passion Business to Touch the Ideal Market**

1.  Have you developed a strategic implementation plan for launch?

2.  Have you set up your fundamental marketing and sales system and process?

3.  Have you designed and built your ideal marketing funnels?

4.  Have you launched your passion business with innovative product and program?

5.  Have you turned your signature program evergreen?

**STEP 7. Expansion: Attract More Ideal Clients and Monetize Your Passion Business**

1.  Have you developed your heart-centered networking, marketing, and social media strategies?

2.  Are you keeping nurturing your leads list and building up influence and loyalty with your expertise?

3.  Have you mastered the Law of Attraction to magnify your ideal clients and prosperity?

4.  Have you applied the best Joint Venture (JV) strategies to help multiply your market presence and convert more ideal clients quickly?

# ABOUT THE AUTHOR

Abundant Entrepreneurship and Thought Leadership Coach **Spring Zheng** is called to work with visionary entrepreneurs and life changers like coaches, authors, speakers and consultants who are driven by their purposes and passions. She loves empowering them to step up and stand out as confident experts and trusted leaders in their ideal niche with their unique gifts, so that they can create abundant businesses and lifestyles, and also positively impact more lives.

As the Founder of Spring Magic Life Society, Inc., Spring leads and inspires a fast- growing community of abundant entrepreneurs. Whether she is working one-on-one with clients or in intimate live or virtual groups, one thing is certain. She will help you uplift and clarify your vision, claim your purposeful and profitable niche, stand up with your magnetic expert presence, and build abundant leadership with confidence that attracts your ideal clients like magic. Spring is on a mission to help entrepreneurs turn their passion into prosperity and transform more lives by creating abundance for all worldwide.

Spring holds an Executive MBA from Rutgers University and Professional Coaching Certificate from New York University. She has over 23 years of professional experience including performance management with a Fortune 100 company and 10 years of abundance coaching.

It sometimes even surprises Spring herself to be shown mysteriously her unique strength and gift in seeing and empowering people into their abundant vision beyond what they can see for themselves. When their eyes suddenly light up with hope and joy, Spring has worked her magic.

An inspirational speaker on the rise, Spring's contagious passion, radiating wisdom, practical strategies and engaging humor keep empowering audiences to take immediate and consistent actions that generate profound growth in their lives and businesses.

Book Spring for Your Keynote, Workshop, or Breakout Session Today!

Get in touch with Spring at: 646-662-8297, Email: **i@SpringMagicLife.com**.

When Spring is not working with clients, you may find her hiking around the Forest Hills Gardens Community in Queens New York, eating healthy salads or spicy hot pot, enjoying outings with friends, or exploring creative activities and having fun with her family and two lovely children.

To learn more please visit: www.SpringMagicLife.com. Connect with Spring on Facebook: https://www.facebook.com/springzheng.

# ACKNOWLEDGMENTS

Great things are never created by chance, or only by any individual.

This is definitely the last but not the least part of this book.

When I sat down to make note of all the people for whom I am so grateful, I felt I could write a whole new chapter!

In my over dozens of years of life experience, and especially in the recent 10 years of accelerated learning and coaching practice, there have been countless people who have contributed to my growth. I won't be able to list and acknowledge them all, but I'd like to start close to home with the people who have touched my life most deeply.

First, my family. I take my life as a magical creation of my parents (my mom Zhi Tai Chen and my dad Xian Chong Zheng) and God, even though my parents got divorced when I just entered into university. I guess the more conflicts inside and outside of me, and the more struggles I have been experiencing, the better I have eventually become, and was able to reach the land of abundance.

Thanks to my husband Yu Xi Liu, my first love since my college years. Your presence and especially the struggles I have been going through for you have been reminding me my original love and faith. You seem to be The Biggest Test for me from God. Thanks for your continuous support through the years, especially support for me to pursue my dreams, providing stable finance for our family, sharing parenting of our two kids, giving mental support for me to take challenges, and helping me review my important work including editing this book. You are super talented and intelligent with independent and critical thinking, the very quality that has attracted me since the beginning. I have endless thanks and prayers that you could hear your greater calling as well and put your talents into the most valuable usage to help make this world a better place.

To my two children Ambrose and Athenia, nothing is more enjoyable than watching your daily growth in all areas, physical, emotional, mental and spiritual. You bring me the best opportunities to love more and become a better person and mom every day. Because of you, I could understand the biggest joy of creation in love, the secret of our greatest Creator. Thanks for being the best blessings of my life. It's always my greatest joy and honor to grow together with you every day!

To Linda Ng who has patiently and efficiently helped me proofread and edit this book. Your timely correction and feedback have greatly helped me improve the quality of this book. I really admire your talents and gentle heart. I am grateful for our growing friendship and our kids' genuine friendships as well.

Thanks to my community of Abundant Entrepreneurs, our vision builders and life changers, our dream pursuers and change makers. We've been interacting on Facebook, LinkedIn, emails, live events and meetups. You and what you have been bravely pursuing make what I have been doing more meaningful. Your appreciation and support make my daily work a more interesting and inspiring experience. Thanks for sharing the passionate entrepreneurship and life fulfillment journey together!

To those great mentors, masters and inspiring influencers, Tony Robbins, Russell Brunson, Brendon Burchard, John Maxwell, Oprah Winfrey, Celine Dion, Joel Osteen, Les Brown, Marie Forleo, Vishen Lakhiani, Kim and Robert Kiyosaki, Dean Graziosi, Kendall SummerHawk, Lisa Sasevich, Clint Arthur, Rich German, Adam Urbanski, Milana Leshinsky, Ed Mylett, Myron Golden, Mirela Sula, and so many more. Thanks to your brave pioneering and innovation in your genius zones, and your great teaching and empowerment through your passionate services. I am always motivated and inspired by your walking ahead of me. Your beings keep me humble and thirsty to learn. Thanks for your unstoppable efforts and role modeling!

These following positive and great-quality communities have greatly impacted me through my growth since early stages and my entrepreneurship journey: my early schools in my hometown with alumni groups who are still in touch, Right Management, Practical Philosophy School in Manhattan, the Business School of Rutgers University, New York University Coaching program, New Life Fellowship Church, Joint Venture Insiders Circle, SASSY Mastermind Group, Global Woman Club, New Life Entrepreneurs Meetup Group, Clickfunnels Two Comma Club and Mastermind Group, World Financial Group Champion Team and Everest Team, GoalCast, MindValley, MindTools, and so many more. I'd thank those leaders who have created these wonderful communities and movements that have been benefiting many more people than the members.

I know there will be more great people, friends, mentors and communities that I will associate with through my exploration and learning. My journey is blessed to be full of surprising discoveries and gratitude.

For all of those and unlimited reasons, I would say Thanks to my Creator, my God. I know that all are from You, and You are for all. I thank everyone who God brings into my life to help me and teach me, and I thank everyone who God gives me the opportunity to love and serve.

I am closing this book with full of peace, joy and gratitude, both inside the book, and inside my heart. May abundance be with you everywhere on every day. Should you miss it somewhere somehow, go create it for your day and make your life a greater masterpiece!

**Spring Magic Life Society, Inc.**

*Abundant Passion, Love, Wisdom, Happiness, Leadership and Success on Purpose...... Coaching, Mentoring, Speaking, Teaching, Mastermind Groups*

# Abundance Train

## 7 Simple Steps To Abundant Life, Business and Impact

## Spring Zheng

Abundant Entrepreneurship and Thought Leadership Coach

*Empowering Visionary Entrepreneurs and Life Changers to Stand Out as Confident Experts and Leaders in their Ideal Niche with their Unique Gifts!*

www.SpringMagicLife.com

www.ingramcontent.com/pod-product-compliance
Lightning Source LLC
Chambersburg PA
CBHW030817180526
45163CB00003B/1318